Wiltshire Trig Baggers Chal

Trig points, or trigonometrical stations to give them th(
common sight and much-loved feature of Britain's hills. Constructeu ᴜᴇᴛᴡᴇᴇ..
1962 as part of the Ordnance Survey's Retriangulation of Great Britain, this log book
is your ideal hiking companion as you 'bag' them all in Wiltshire.

Keeping a logbook is great for reminiscing about your adventures, share your hikes
with friends and family - tick off the list as you complete the challenges one by one.
This log book contains 103 trig pillars in and around Wiltshire, so get your hiking
ᴜᴜᴜᴛs ᴜɴ and take on the Wiltshire Trig Bagger Challenge!

How to use this logbook...

Use the map page to select the trigs you are
planning to climb, then identify the trig in the
contents page.

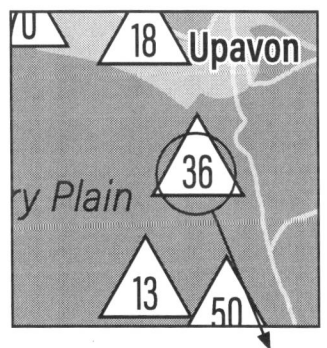

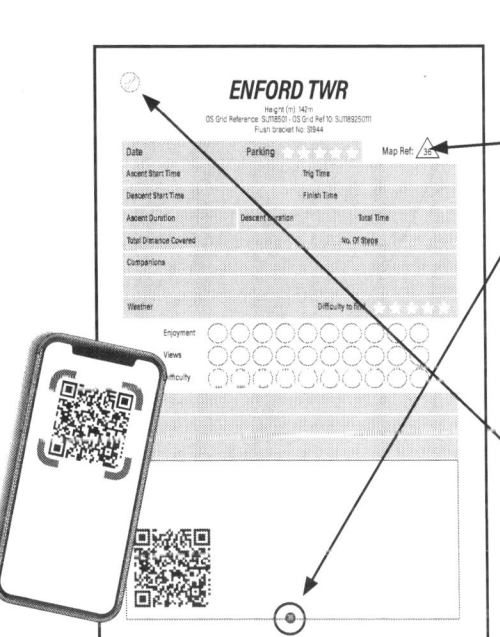

Go to the trig logbook page, then
scan the QR code to open a trig map
on your smartphone so you can
plan your route. Note the OS grid
reference which you can enter into
your GPS system to follow on the day.

Record your adventure
and tick off the trig when
you're done!

TOP TIP:
You can zoom in and out on the map on your phone
by pressing the [+] and [-] buttons. Take screenshots
in case you are out of mobile data on the hills.

Hiking can be dangerous without proper planning and preparation, this activity is taken at your own risk. Please equip yourself with necessary supplies/equipment
for your adventure and notify friends or relatives in advance of your hike and your planned route. All trig information and locations correct at time of printing.

Trig Finder - At a glance

Scan the QR code to open the Trigs on your smartphone

1. ALDBOURNE GORSE	37. ETCHILHAMPTON HILL	73. SILK HILL
2. BAKE BARN	38. FIR HILL	74. STOCKTON
3. BARFORD DOWN	39. FLAXLANDS RESR	75. STRIDES ROW
4. BARROW STREET	40. FOSBURY CAMP	76. SUTTON DOWN
5. BATTERY HILL	41. FURZE HEDGE BARN	77. TAN HILL
6. BATTLESBURY HILL	42. GIANTS GRAVE	78. TEFFONT DOWN
7. BEACON HILL	43. GROVELY CASTLE	79. TERRACE HILL
8. BISHOPSTONE DOWN	44. GROVELY HILL	80. THRUXTON DOWN
9. BOTLEY DOWN	45. HACKPEN HILL	81. TITTLE PATH HILL
10. BRADENSTOKE	46. HORNINGSHAM	82. TRIPLE PLANTATION
11. BRADLEY KNOLL	47. INHAM DOWN	83. TROW DOWN
12. BRAMSHAW	48. INKPEN HILL	84. UPTON COW DOWN
13. BUSTARD	49. KENTSWOOD	85. WADEN HILL
14. CASTLE COMBE	50. KNIGHTON DOWN	86. WADSWICK
15. CASTLE DITCHES	51. KNOOK BARROW	87. WARMINSTER BOTTOM
16. CAUSEWAY	52. LIDDINGTON CASTLE	88. WEST HILL
17. CHARLBURY HILL	53. LITTLE HILL	89. WEST KNOYLE TUMULUS
18. CHARLTON CLUMPS	54. MARKET LAVINGTON	90. WEST WELLOW
19. CHESSLEY HILL	55. MARTINSELL	91. WESTBURY DOWN
20. CLAYPIT HILL	56. MELBURY HILL	92. WEXCOMBE DOWN
21. CLEARBURY RING	57. MILTON HILL	93. WHITE SHEET CASTLE
22. CLEVERTON	58. MORGANS HILL	94. WHITE SHEET HILL
23. CLEY HILL	59. NEBO FARM	95. WICK DOWN
24. CODFORD CIRCLE	60. PALE ASH	96. WICK DOWN
25. COLD KITCHEN	61. PENNING FIELD	97. WINGREEN
26. COMBE FARM RESR	62. PENTRIDGE HILL	98. WINTERSLOW
27. COMPTON HUT	63. PICKED HILL	99. WOODFORD
28. COPEHILL	64. PICKPIT HILL	100. WORTHY HILL FARM
29. CORTON DOWN	65. POULTON DOWNS	101. WORTON
30. CROOKED SOLEY	66. POUND BOTTOM	102. WROUGHTON
31. CROUCH DOWN	67. PRESHUTE	103. YARNBURY CASTLE
32. DAMERHAM KNOLL	68. PYT HOUSE	
33. DUNCLIFFE HILL	69. QUARLEY CAMP	
34. EAST DEAN	70. REDHORN HILL	
35. EAST ORCHARD	71. ROYAL OAK	
36. ENFORD TWR	72. SIDBURY	

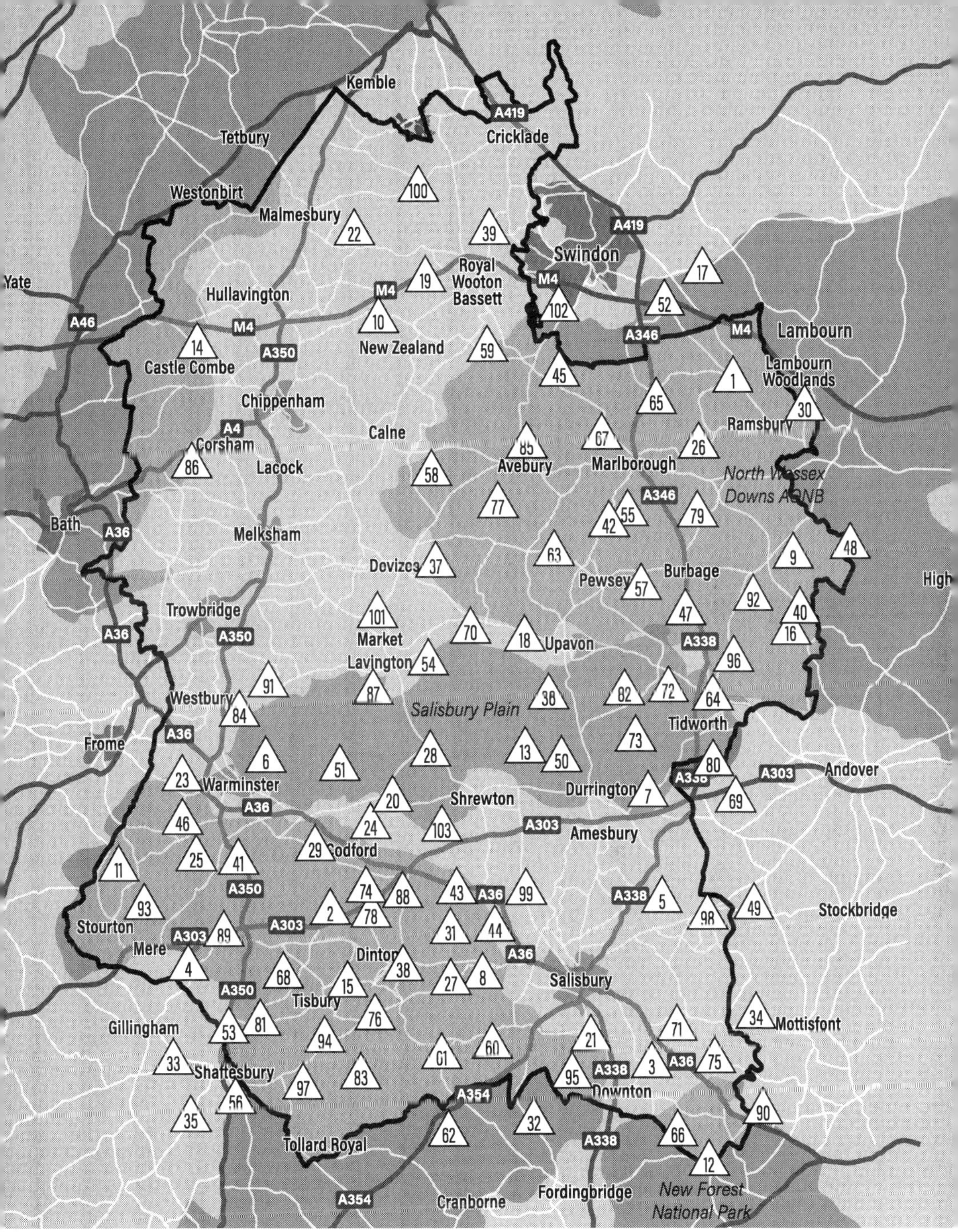

Salisbury Plain Training Area

The public has access except when the Range Danger Areas are in use for live firing. Firing times must be checked & warning signals (red flags during day or red lamps at night) must be heeded.

More information can be obtained from:
www.gov.uk/government/publications/
salisbury-plain-training-area-spta-firing-times

Scan me for interactive map

Trig Tick Offs- In Alphabetical Order

✓	Hill Name	Page	✓	Hill Name	Page
○	ALDBOURNE GORSE	Page 1	○	ENFORD TWR	Page 36
○	BAKE BARN	Page 2	○	ETCHILHAMPTON HILL	Page 37
○	BARFORD DOWN	Page 3	○	FIR HILL	Page 38
○	BARROW STREET	Page 4	○	FLAXLANDS RESR	Page 39
○	BATTERY HILL	Page 5	○	FOSBURY CAMP	Page 40
○	BATTLESBURY HILL	Page 6	○	FURZE HEDGE BARN	Page 41
○	BEACON HILL	Page 7	○	GIANTS GRAVE	Page 42
○	BISHOPSTONE DOWN	Page 8	○	GROVELY CASTLE	Page 43
○	BOTLEY DOWN	Page 9	○	GROVELY HILL	Page 44
○	BRADENSTOKE	Page 10	○	HACKPEN HILL	Page 45
○	BRADLEY KNOLL	Page 11	○	HORNINGSHAM	Page 46
○	BRAMSHAW	Page 12	○	INHAM DOWN	Page 47
○	BUSTARD	Page 13	○	INKPEN HILL	Page 48
○	CASTLE COMBE	Page 14	○	KENTSWOOD	Page 49
○	CASTLE DITCHES	Page 15	○	KNIGHTON DOWN	Page 50
○	CAUSEWAY	Page 16	○	KNOOK BARROW	Page 51
○	CHARLBURY HILL	Page 17	○	LIDDINGTON CASTLE	Page 52
○	CHARLTON CLUMPS	Page 18	○	LITTLE HILL	Page 53
○	CHESSLEY HILL	Page 19	○	MARKET LAVINGTON	Page 54
○	CLAYPIT HILL	Page 20	○	MARTINSELL	Page 55
○	CLEARBURY RING	Page 21	○	MELBURY HILL	Page 56
○	CLEVERTON	Page 22	○	MILTON HILL	Page 57
○	CLEY HILL	Page 23	○	MORGANS HILL	Page 58
○	CODFORD CIRCLE	Page 24	○	NEBO FARM	Page 59
○	COLD KITCHEN	Page 25	○	PALE ASH	Page 60
○	COMBE FARM RESR	Page 26	○	PENNING FIELD	Page 61
○	COMPTON HUT	Page 27	○	PENTRIDGE HILL	Page 62
○	COPEHILL	Page 28	○	PICKED HILL	Page 63
○	CORTON DOWN	Page 29	○	PICKPIT HILL	Page 64
○	CROOKED SOLEY	Page 30	○	POULTON DOWNS	Page 65
○	CROUCH DOWN	Page 31	○	POUND BOTTOM	Page 66
○	DAMERHAM KNOLL	Page 32	○	PRESHUTE	Page 67
○	DUNCLIFFE HILL	Page 33	○	PYT HOUSE	Page 68
○	EAST DEAN	Page 34	○	QUARLEY CAMP	Page 69
○	EAST ORCHARD	Page 35	○	REDHORN HILL	Page 70

✓ Hill Name	Page
○ ROYAL OAK	Page 71
○ SIDBURY	Page 72
○ SILK HILL	Page 73
○ STOCKTON	Page 74
○ STRIDES ROW	Page 75
○ SUTTON DOWN	Page 76
○ TAN HILL	Page 77
○ TEFFONT DOWN	Page 78
○ TERRACE HILL	Page 79
○ THRUXTON DOWN	Page 80
○ TITTLE PATH HILL	Page 81
○ TRIPLE PLANTATION	Page 82
○ TROW DOWN	Page 83
○ UPTON COW DOWN	Page 84
○ WADEN HILL	Page 85
○ WADSWICK	Page 86
○ WARMINSTER BOTTOM	Page 87
○ WEST HILL	Page 88
○ WEST KNOYLE TUMULUS	Page 89
○ WEST WELLOW	Page 90
○ WESTBURY DOWN	Page 91
○ WEXCOMBE DOWN	Page 92
○ WHITE SHEET CASTLE	Page 93
○ WHITE SHEET HILL	Page 94
○ WICK DOWN	Page 95
○ WICK DOWN	Page 96
○ WINGREEN	Page 97
○ WINTERSLOW	Page 98
○ WOODFORD	Page 99
○ WORTHY HILL FARM	Page 100
○ WORTON	Page 101
○ WROUGHTON	Page 102
○ YARNBURY CASTLE	Page 103

Trig Finder - In Height Ascending Order

45 m	WEST WELLOW	Page 90
81 m	STRIDES ROW	Page 75
85 m	WORTON	Page 101
100 m	CLEVERTON	Page 22
105 m	DAMERHAM KNOLL	Page 32
110 m	BARFORD DOWN	Page 3
112 m	EAST DEAN	Page 34
115 m	WICK DOWN	Page 95
118 m	BARROW STREET	Page 4
118 m	EAST ORCHARD	Page 35
125 m	BRAMSHAW	Page 12
125 m	POUND BOTTOM	Page 66
130 m	CROUCH DOWN	Page 31
131 m	KENTSWOOD	Page 49
135 m	WORTHY HILL FARM	Page 100
136 m	CHESSLEY HILL	Page 19
138 m	CASTLE COMBE	Page 14
138 m	WADSWICK	Page 86
139 m	COPEHILL	Page 28
141 m	BUSTARD	Page 13
142 m	CLEARBURY RING	Page 21
142 m	ENFORD TWR	Page 36
143 m	SILK HILL	Page 73
143 m	TRIPLE PLANTATION	Page 82
144 m	GROVELY HILL	Page 44
147 m	KNIGHTON DOWN	Page 50
156 m	GROVELY CASTLE	Page 43
156 m	WOODFORD	Page 99
157 m	BRADENSTOKE	Page 10
157 m	FLAXLANDS RESR	Page 39
157 m	ROYAL OAK	Page 71
159 m	BATTERY HILL	Page 5
159 m	FIR HILL	Page 38
163 m	WINTERSLOW	Page 98
167 m	YARNBURY CASTLE	Page 103
170 m	PALE ASH	Page 60
170 m	QUARLEY CAMP	Page 69
172 m	TEFFONT DOWN	Page 78
173 m	PICKPIT HILL	Page 64
174 m	BAKE BARN	Page 2
174 m	THRUXTON DOWN	Page 80
176 m	HORNINGSHAM	Page 46
179 m	CLAYPIT HILL	Page 20
181 m	BISHOPSTONE DOWN	Page 8
183 m	COMBE FARM RESR	Page 26
185 m	PENTRIDGE HILL	Page 62
185 m	WICK DOWN	Page 96
188 m	CODFORD CIRCLE	Page 24
188 m	CORTON DOWN	Page 29
188 m	SIDBURY	Page 72
189 m	KNOOK BARROW	Page 51
189 m	WARMINSTER BOTTOM	Page 87
190 m	CHARLTON CLUMPS	Page 18
190 m	ETCHILHAMPTON HILL	Page 37
192 m	WADEN HILL	Page 85
193 m	CASTLE DITCHES	Page 15
193 m	COMPTON HUT	Page 27
195 m	MARKET LAVINGTON	Page 54
196 m	INHAM DOWN	Page 47
196 m	PRESHUTE	Page 67
196 m	STOCKTON	Page 74
196 m	TERRACE HILL	Page 79
197 m	PENNING FIELD	Page 61
198 m	WEST HILL	Page 88
200 m	UPTON COW DOWN	Page 84
202 m	PICKED HILL	Page 63
204 m	BEACON HILL	Page 7
208 m	BATTLESBURY HILL	Page 6
208 m	WROUGHTON	Page 102
210 m	DUNCLIFFE HILL	Page 33
213 m	REDHORN HILL	Page 70
213 m	SUTTON DOWN	Page 76
214 m	ALDBOURNE GORSE	Page 1
214 m	CROOKED SOLEY	Page 30
214 m	PYT HOUSE	Page 68
215 m	NEBO FARM	Page 59
221 m	POULTON DOWNS	Page 65
226 m	BOTLEY DOWN	Page 9
228 m	WEST KNOYLE TUMULUS	Page 89
230 m	WESTBURY DOWN	Page 91
238 m	FURZE HEDGE BARN	Page 41
239 m	CLEY HILL	Page 23
239 m	MILTON HILL	Page 57
242 m	TITTLE PATH HILL	Page 81
243 m	WHITE SHEET HILL	Page 94
244 m	TROW DOWN	Page 83
245 m	WHITE SHEET CASTLE	Page 93
249 m	LITTLE HILL	Page 53
250 m	GIANTS GRAVE	Page 42
251 m	CAUSEWAY	Page 16
253 m	CHARLBURY HILL	Page 17
258 m	COLD KITCHEN	Page 25
258 m	FOSBURY CAMP	Page 40
260 m	MORGANS HILL	Page 58
263 m	MELBURY HILL	Page 56
267 m	WEXCOMBE DOWN	Page 92
272 m	HACKPEN HILL	Page 45
278 m	LIDDINGTON CASTLE	Page 52
278 m	WINGREEN	Page 97
288 m	BRADLEY KNOLL	Page 11
290 m	INKPEN HILL	Page 48
290 m	MARTINSELL	Page 55
294 m	TAN HILL	Page 77

ALDBOURNE GORSE

Height (m): 214m
OS Grid Reference: SU263739 • OS Grid Ref 10: SU2635073950
Flush bracket No: S2404

Date	Parking ★★★★★	Map Ref: /1\

Ascent Start Time / **Trig Time**

Descent Start Time / **Finish Time**

Ascent Duration / **Descent Duration** / **Total Time**

Total Distance Covered / **No. Of Steps**

Companions

Weather / **Difficulty to find** ★★★★★

Enjoyment ○○○○○○○○○○
Views ○○○○○○○○○○
Difficulty ○○○○○○○○○○

Highlights

Notes

BAKE BARN

Height (m): 174m
OS Grid Reference: ST949340 • OS Grid Ref 10: ST9495034050
Flush bracket No: S2199

| Date | Parking ★★★★★ | Map Ref: 2 |

Ascent Start Time	Trig Time
Descent Start Time	Finish Time
Ascent Duration	Descent Duration	Total Time
Total Distance Covered	No. Of Steps
Companions	

| Weather | Difficulty to find ★★★★★ |

- Enjoyment ○○○○○○○○○○
- Views ○○○○○○○○○○
- Difficulty ○○○○○○○○○○

Highlights

Notes

BARFORD DOWN

Height (m): 110m
OS Grid Reference: SU197224 • OS Grid Ref 10: SU1974822400
Flush bracket No: S2605

Date	Parking ☆☆☆☆☆	Map Ref: /3\
Ascent Start Time	Trig Time	
Descent Start Time	Finish Time	
Ascent Duration	Descent Duration	Total Time
Total Distance Covered		No. Of Steps
Companions		

Weather

Difficulty to find ☆☆☆☆☆

Enjoyment ○○○○○○○○○○
Views ○○○○○○○○○○
Difficulty ○○○○○○○○○○

Highlights

Notes

BARROW STREET

Height (m): 118m
OS Grid Reference: ST838301 • OS Grid Ref 10: ST8381230184
Flush bracket No: S2225

Date	Parking ★★★★★	Map Ref: 4
Ascent Start Time		Trig Time
Descent Start Time		Finish Time
Ascent Duration	Descent Duration	Total Time
Total Distance Covered		No. Of Steps
Companions		

Weather

Difficulty to find ★★★★★

Enjoyment ○○○○○○○○○○
Views ○○○○○○○○○○
Difficulty ○○○○○○○○○○

Highlights

Notes

BATTERY HILL

Height (m): 159m
OS Grid Reference: SU206348 • OS Grid Ref 10: SU2062634846
Flush bracket No: S2617

Date	Parking ☆☆☆☆☆	Map Ref: 5
Ascent Start Time	Trig Time	
Descent Start Time	Finish Time	
Ascent Duration	Descent Duration	Total Time
Total Distance Covered	No. Of Steps	
Companions		

Weather

Difficulty to find ☆☆☆☆☆

Enjoyment ○○○○○○○○○○
Views ○○○○○○○○○○
Difficulty ○○○○○○○○○○

Highlights

Notes

BATTLESBURY HILL

Height (m): 208m
OS Grid Reference: ST898455 • OS Grid Ref 10: ST8988545548
Flush bracket No: S2174

Date	Parking ★★★★★	Map Ref: 6

Ascent Start Time | Trig Time

Descent Start Time | Finish Time

Ascent Duration | Descent Duration | Total Time

Total Distance Covered | No. Of Steps

Companions

Weather | Difficulty to find ★★★★★

Enjoyment ○○○○○○○○○○
Views ○○○○○○○○○○
Difficulty ○○○○○○○○○○

Highlights

Notes

BEACON HILL

Height (m): 204m
OS Grid Reference: SU195427 • OS Grid Ref 10: SU1950042749
Flush bracket No: S1504

Date	Parking ★★★★★	Map Ref: /7\

Ascent Start Time	Trig Time

Descent Start Time	Finish Time

Ascent Duration	Descent Duration	Total Time

Total Distance Covered	No. Of Steps

Companions

Weather	Difficulty to find ★★★★★

Enjoyment ○○○○○○○○○○
Views ○○○○○○○○○○
Difficulty ○○○○○○○○○○

Highlights

Notes

BISHOPSTONE DOWN

Height (m): 181m
OS Grid Reference: SU066292 • OS Grid Ref 10: SU0669629207
Flush bracket No: S2209

| Date | Parking ★★★★★ | Map Ref: 8 |

Ascent Start Time | Trig Time

Descent Start Time | Finish Time

Ascent Duration | Descent Duration | Total Time

Total Distance Covered | No. Of Steps

Companions

Weather | Difficulty to find ★★★★★

Enjoyment ○○○○○○○○○○
Views ○○○○○○○○○○
Difficulty ○○○○○○○○○○

Highlights

Notes

BOTLEY DOWN

Height (m): 226m
OS Grid Reference: SU308609 • OS Grid Ref 10: SU3080560958
Flush bracket No: S1908

Date	Parking ★★★★★	Map Ref: 9
Ascent Start Time		Trig Time
Descent Start Time		Finish Time
Ascent Duration	Descent Duration	Total Time
Total Distance Covered		No. Of Steps
Companions		
Weather		Difficulty to find ★★★★★

Enjoyment ○○○○○○○○○
Views ○○○○○○○○○
Difficulty ○○○○○○○○○

Highlights

Notes

BRADENSTOKE

Height (m): 157m
OS Grid Reference: ST990784 • OS Grid Ref 10: ST9909178467
Flush bracket No: S2397

Date	Parking ★★★★★	Map Ref: /10
Ascent Start Time		Trig Time
Descent Start Time		Finish Time
Ascent Duration	Descent Duration	Total Time
Total Distance Covered		No. Of Steps
Companions		

Weather		Difficulty to find ★★★★★

Enjoyment ○○○○○○○○○○
Views ○○○○○○○○○○
Difficulty ○○○○○○○○○○

Highlights

Notes

BRADLEY KNOLL

Height (m): 288m
OS Grid Reference: ST785376 • OS Grid Ref 10: ST7859837649
Flush bracket No: S1514

Date	Parking ☆☆☆☆☆	Map Ref: /11\
Ascent Start Time		Trig Time
Descent Start Time		Finish Time
Ascent Duration	Descent Duration	Total Time
Total Distance Covered		No. Of Steps
Companions		

Weather

Difficulty to find ☆☆☆☆☆

Enjoyment ○○○○○○○○○○
Views   ○○○○○○○○○○
Difficulty ○○○○○○○○○○

Highlights

Notes

BRAMSHAW

Height (m): 125m
OS Grid Reference: SU244151 • OS Grid Ref 10: SU2445115123
Flush bracket No: S2718

Date	Parking ★★★★★	Map Ref: /12\

Ascent Start Time	Trig Time

Descent Start Time	Finish Time

Ascent Duration	Descent Duration	Total Time

Total Distance Covered	No. Of Steps

Companions

Weather | Difficulty to find ★★★★★

Enjourment ○○○○○○○○○○
Views ○○○○○○○○○○
Difficulty ○○○○○○○○○○

Highlights

Notes

BUSTARD

Height (m): 141m
OS Grid Reference: SU101461 • OS Grid Ref 10: SU1011646104
Flush bracket No: S1949

Date	Parking ★★★★★	Map Ref: /13\
Ascent Start Time		Trig Time
Descent Start Time		Finish Time
Ascent Duration	Descent Duration	Total Time
Total Distance Covered		No. Of Steps
Companions		

Weather

Difficulty to find ★★★★★

Enjoyment ○○○○○○○○○○
Views ○○○○○○○○○○
Difficulty ○○○○○○○○○○

Highlights

Notes

CASTLE COMBE

Height (m): 138m
OS Grid Reference: ST847765 • OS Grid Ref 10: ST8471176529
Flush bracket No: S2504

Date	Parking ★★★★★	Map Ref: /14\

Ascent Start Time	Trig Time

Descent Start Time	Finish Time

Ascent Duration	Descent Duration	Total Time

Total Distance Covered	No. Of Steps

Companions

Weather	Difficulty to find ★★★★★

Enjoyment ○○○○○○○○○○
Views ○○○○○○○○○○
Difficulty ○○○○○○○○○○

Highlights

Notes

CASTLE DITCHES

Height (m): 193m
OS Grid Reference: ST962284 • OS Grid Ref 10: ST9623028497
Flush bracket No: S2221

Date	Parking ☆☆☆☆☆	Map Ref: /15\
Ascent Start Time		Trig Time
Descent Start Time		Finish Time
Ascent Duration	Descent Duration	Total Time
Total Distance Covered		No. Of Steps
Companions		

| Weather | | Difficulty to find ☆☆☆☆☆ |

Enjoyment ○○○○○○○○○○
Views ○○○○○○○○○○
Difficulty ○○○○○○○○○○

Highlights

Notes

CAUSEWAY

Height (m): 251m
OS Grid Reference: SU309553 • OS Grid Ref 10: SU3095955303
Flush bracket No: S1698

Date	Parking ★★★★★	Map Ref: 16

Ascent Start Time | **Trig Time**

Descent Start Time | **Finish Time**

Ascent Duration | **Descent Duration** | **Total Time**

Total Distance Covered | **No. Of Steps**

Companions

Weather | **Difficulty to find** ★★★★★

Enjoyment ○○○○○○○○○○
Views ○○○○○○○○○○
Difficulty ○○○○○○○○○○

Highlights

Notes

CHARLBURY HILL

Height (m): 253m
OS Grid Reference: SU237821 • OS Grid Ref 10: SU2378282116
Flush bracket No: S2435

Date	Parking ☆☆☆☆☆	Map Ref: 17

Ascent Start Time	Trig Time

Descent Start Time	Finish Time

Ascent Duration	Descent Duration	Total Time

Total Distance Covered	No. Of Steps

Companions

Weather	Difficulty to find ☆☆☆☆☆

Enjoyment ○○○○○○○○○○
Views ○○○○○○○○○○
Difficulty ○○○○○○○○○○

Highlights

Notes

CHARLTON CLUMPS

Height (m): 190m
OS Grid Reference: SU102545 • OS Grid Ref 10: SU1020854575
Flush bracket No: S1943

Date	Parking ★★★★★	Map Ref: /18\

Ascent Start Time	Trig Time

Descent Start Time	Finish Time

Ascent Duration	Descent Duration	Total Time

Total Distance Covered	No. Of Steps

Companions

Weather	Difficulty to find ★★★★★

Enjoyment ○○○○○○○○○○
Views ○○○○○○○○○○
Difficulty ○○○○○○○○○○

Highlights

Notes

CHESSLEY HILL

Height (m): 136m
OS Grid Reference: SU026816 • OS Grid Ref 10: SU0262181669
Flush bracket No: S2399

Date	Parking ★★★★★	Map Ref: /19\
Ascent Start Time		Trig Time
Descent Start Time		Finish Time
Ascent Duration	Descent Duration	Total Time
Total Distance Covered		No. Of Steps
Companions		
Weather		Difficulty to find ★★★★★

Enjoration ○○○○○○○○○○
Views ○○○○○○○○○○
Difficulty ○○○○○○○○○○

Highlights

Notes

CLAYPIT HILL

Height (m): 179m
OS Grid Reference: ST996424 • OS Grid Ref 10: ST9968242453
Flush bracket No: S1941

Date	Parking ★★★★★	Map Ref: /20\
Ascent Start Time		Trig Time
Descent Start Time		Finish Time
Ascent Duration	Descent Duration	Total Time
Total Distance Covered		No. Of Steps
Companions		

| Weather | | Difficulty to find ★★★★★ |

Enjoyment ○○○○○○○○○
Views ○○○○○○○○○
Difficulty ○○○○○○○○○

Highlights

Notes

CLEARBURY RING

Height (m): 142m
OS Grid Reference: SU152245 • OS Grid Ref 10: SU1524124526
Flush bracket No: S2608

Date	Parking ★★★★★	Map Ref: /21
Ascent Start Time		Trig Time
Descent Start Time		Finish Time
Ascent Duration	Descent Duration	Total Time
Total Distance Covered		No. Of Steps
Companions		
Weather		Difficulty to find ★★★★★

Enjoyment ○○○○○○○○○○
Views ○○○○○○○○○○
Difficulty ○○○○○○○○○○

Highlights

Notes

CLEVERTON

Height (m): 100m
OS Grid Reference: ST971849 • OS Grid Ref 10: ST9711484975
Flush bracket No: S2419

| Date | Parking ☆☆☆☆☆ | Map Ref: /22\ |

| Ascent Start Time | Trig Time |

| Descent Start Time | Finish Time |

| Ascent Duration | Descent Duration | Total Time |

| Total Distance Covered | No. Of Steps |

| Companions |

| Weather | Difficulty to find ★★★★★ |

Enjoyment ○○○○○○○○○○
Views ○○○○○○○○○○
Difficulty ○○○○○○○○○○

Highlights

Notes

CLEY HILL

Height (m): 239m
OS Grid Reference: ST837449 • OS Grid Ref 10: ST8379144989
Flush bracket No: S2533

| Date | Parking ☆☆☆☆☆ | Map Ref: 23 |

Ascent Start Time	Trig Time
Descent Start Time	Finish Time
Ascent Duration	Descent Duration	Total Time
Total Distance Covered	No. Of Steps
Companions	

| Weather | Difficulty to find ☆☆☆☆☆ |

Enjoyment ○○○○○○○○○○
Views ○○○○○○○○○○
Difficulty ○○○○○○○○○○

Highlights

Notes

CODFORD CIRCLE

Height (m): 188m
OS Grid Reference: ST982405 • OS Grid Ref 10: ST9825440556
Flush bracket No: S2171

| Date | Parking ★★★★★ | Map Ref: /24\ |

Ascent Start Time		Trig Time	
Descent Start Time		Finish Time	
Ascent Duration	Descent Duration	Total Time
Total Distance Covered		No. Of Steps	
Companions			

Weather | Difficulty to find ★★★★★

Enjoyment ○○○○○○○○○○
Views ○○○○○○○○○○
Difficulty ○○○○○○○○○○

Highlights

Notes

COLD KITCHEN

Height (m): 258m
OS Grid Reference: ST845382 • OS Grid Ref 10: ST8457338249
Flush bracket No: S2183

Date	Parking ★★★★★	Map Ref: /25\

Ascent Start Time	Trig Time

Descent Start Time	Finish Time

Ascent Duration	Descent Duration	Total Time

Total Distance Covered	No. Of Steps

Companions

Weather | **Difficulty to find** ★★★★★

Enjoyment ○○○○○○○○○○
Views ○○○○○○○○○○
Difficulty ○○○○○○○○○○

Highlights

Notes

COMBE FARM RESR

Height (m): 183m
OS Grid Reference: SU235690 • OS Grid Ref 10: SU2350169007
Flush bracket No: S2405

| Date | Parking ★★★★★ | Map Ref: /26\ |

Ascent Start Time | Trig Time

Descent Start Time | Finish Time

Ascent Duration | Descent Duration | Total Time

Total Distance Covered | No. Of Steps

Companions

Weather | Difficulty to find ★★★★★

Enjoyment ○○○○○○○○○
Views ○○○○○○○○○
Difficulty ○○○○○○○○○

Highlights

Notes

COMPTON HUT

Height (m): 193m
OS Grid Reference: SU042288 • OS Grid Ref 10: SU0427428888
Flush bracket No: S2210

| Date | Parking ☆☆☆☆☆ | Map Ref: 27 |

Ascent Start Time | **Trig Time**

Descent Start Time | **Finish Time**

Ascent Duration | **Descent Duration** | **Total Time**

Total Distance Covered | **No. Of Steps**

Companions

Weather | **Difficulty to find** ☆☆☆☆☆

Enjoyment ○○○○○○○○○○
Views ○○○○○○○○○○
Difficulty ○○○○○○○○○○

Highlights

Notes

COPEHILL

Height (m): 139m
OS Grid Reference: SU027460 • OS Grid Ref 10: SU0277646094
Flush bracket No: S1939

| Date | Parking ★ ★ ★ ★ ★ | Map Ref: 28 |

Ascent Start Time | Trig Time

Descent Start Time | Finish Time

Ascent Duration | Descent Duration | Total Time

Total Distance Covered | No. Of Steps

Companions

Weather | Difficulty to find ★ ★ ★ ★ ★

Enjoyment ◯ ◯ ◯ ◯ ◯ ◯ ◯ ◯ ◯ ◯
Views   ◯ ◯ ◯ ◯ ◯ ◯ ◯ ◯ ◯ ◯
Difficulty ◯ ◯ ◯ ◯ ◯ ◯ ◯ ◯ ◯ ◯

Highlights

Notes

CORTON DOWN

Height (m): 188m
OS Grid Reference: ST938388 • OS Grid Ref 10: ST9380738878
Flush bracket No: S2187

Date	Parking ☆☆☆☆☆	Map Ref: /29\
Ascent Start Time		Trig Time
Descent Start Time		Finish Time
Ascent Duration	Descent Duration	Total Time
Total Distance Covered		No. Of Steps
Companions		

Weather		Difficulty to find ☆☆☆☆☆

Enjoyment ○○○○○○○○○○
Views ○○○○○○○○○○
Difficulty ○○○○○○○○○○

Highlights

Notes

CROOKED SOLEY

Height (m): 214m
OS Grid Reference: SU315719 • OS Grid Ref 10: SU3157571963
Flush bracket No: 11395

Date	Parking ☆☆☆☆☆	Map Ref: /30\
Ascent Start Time		Trig Time
Descent Start Time		Finish Time
Ascent Duration	Descent Duration	Total Time
Total Distance Covered		No. Of Steps
Companions		

Weather

Difficulty to find ☆☆☆☆☆

Enjoyment ○○○○○○○○○○
Views ○○○○○○○○○○
Difficulty ○○○○○○○○○○

Highlights

Notes

CROUCH DOWN

Height (m): 130m
OS Grid Reference: SU043324 • OS Grid Ref 10: SU0430932473
Flush bracket No: S2204

Date	Parking	Map Ref: 31

Ascent Start Time | **Trig Time**

Descent Start Time | **Finish Time**

Ascent Duration | **Descent Duration** | **Total Time**

Total Distance Covered | **No. Of Steps**

Companions

Weather | **Difficulty to find**

Enjoyment ○○○○○○○○○○
Views ○○○○○○○○○○
Difficulty ○○○○○○○○○○

Highlights

Notes

DAMERHAM KNOLL

Height (m): 105m
OS Grid Reference: SU106181 • OS Grid Ref 10: SU1061018138
Flush bracket No: S2807

Date	Parking ☆☆☆☆☆	Map Ref: /32\

Ascent Start Time | **Trig Time**

Descent Start Time | **Finish Time**

Ascent Duration | **Descent Duration** | **Total Time**

Total Distance Covered | **No. Of Steps**

Companions

Weather | **Difficulty to find** ☆☆☆☆☆

Enjoyment ○○○○○○○○○○
Views ○○○○○○○○○○
Difficulty ○○○○○○○○○○

Highlights

Notes

DUNCLIFFE HILL

Height (m): 210m
OS Grid Reference: ST825225 • OS Grid Ref 10: ST8259522599
Flush bracket No: S6023

Date	Parking ★★★★★	Map Ref: /33\

Ascent Start Time	Trig Time

Descent Start Time	Finish Time

Ascent Duration	Descent Duration	Total Time

Total Distance Covered	No. Of Steps

Companions

Weather	Difficulty to find ★★★★★

Enjoyment ○○○○○○○○○○
Views ○○○○○○○○○○
Difficulty ○○○○○○○○○○

Highlights

Notes

EAST DEAN

Height (m): 112m
OS Grid Reference: SU277260 • OS Grid Ref 10: SU2778626069
Flush bracket No: S2806

Date	Parking	Map Ref: 34

Ascent Start Time | Trig Time

Descent Start Time | Finish Time

Ascent Duration | Descent Duration | Total Time

Total Distance Covered | No. Of Steps

Companions

Weather | Difficulty to find

- Enjoyment
- Views
- Difficulty

Highlights

Notes

EAST ORCHARD

Height (m): 118m
OS Grid Reference: ST839181 • OS Grid Ref 10: ST8396418199
Flush bracket No: S6045

Date	Parking ☆☆☆☆☆	Map Ref: /35\
Ascent Start Time		Trig Time
Descent Start Time		Finish Time
Ascent Duration	Descent Duration	Total Time
Total Distance Covered		No. Of Steps
Companions		

Weather	Difficulty to find ☆☆☆☆☆

Enjoyment ○○○○○○○○○○
Views ○○○○○○○○○○
Difficulty ○○○○○○○○○○

Highlights

Notes

ENFORD TWR

Height (m): 142m
OS Grid Reference: SU118501 · OS Grid Ref 10: SU1189250111
Flush bracket No: S1944

| Date | Parking | Map Ref: /36\ |

Ascent Start Time | Trig Time

Descent Start Time | Finish Time

Ascent Duration | Descent Duration | Total Time

Total Distance Covered | No. Of Steps

Companions

Weather | Difficulty to find ★★★★★

Enjoyment ○○○○○○○○○○
Views ○○○○○○○○○○
Difficulty ○○○○○○○○○○

Highlights

Notes

ETCHILHAMPTON HILL

Height (m): 190m
OS Grid Reference: SU032601 • OS Grid Ref 10: SU0328560142
Flush bracket No: S2502

Date	Parking ☆☆☆☆☆	Map Ref: 37

- Ascent Start Time
- Trig Time
- Descent Start Time
- Finish Time
- Ascent Duration | Descent Duration | Total Time
- Total Distance Covered | No. Of Steps
- Companions

Weather | Difficulty to find ☆☆☆☆☆

Enjoyment ○○○○○○○○○○
Views ○○○○○○○○○○
Difficulty ○○○○○○○○○○

Highlights

Notes

FIR HILL

Height (m): 159m
OS Grid Reference: SU004296 • OS Grid Ref 10: SU0048429677
Flush bracket No: S2212

Date	Parking ★★★★★	Map Ref: /38\
Ascent Start Time		Trig Time
Descent Start Time		Finish Time
Ascent Duration	Descent Duration	Total Time
Total Distance Covered		No. Of Steps
Companions		

Weather | Difficulty to find ★★★★★

Enjoyment ○○○○○○○○○○
Views ○○○○○○○○○○
Difficulty ○○○○○○○○○○

Highlights

Notes

FLAXLANDS RESR

Height (m): 157m
OS Grid Reference: SU075849 • OS Grid Ref 10: SU0751784981
Flush bracket No: S6239

Date	Parking ☆☆☆☆☆	Map Ref: /39\

Ascent Start Time	Trig Time

Descent Start Time	Finish Time

Ascent Duration	Descent Duration	Total Time

Total Distance Covered	No. Of Steps

Companions

Weather — Difficulty to find ☆☆☆☆☆

Enjoyment ○○○○○○○○○○
Views ○○○○○○○○○○
Difficulty ○○○○○○○○○○

Highlights

Notes

FOSBURY CAMP

Height (m): 258m
OS Grid Reference: SU313566 • OS Grid Ref 10: SU3138256677
Flush bracket No: S1703

Date	Parking ★★★★★	Map Ref: /40\
Ascent Start Time		Trig Time
Descent Start Time		Finish Time
Ascent Duration	Descent Duration	Total Time
Total Distance Covered		No. Of Steps
Companions		

Weather | Difficulty to find ★★★★★

Enjoyment ○○○○○○○○○○
Views ○○○○○○○○○○
Difficulty ○○○○○○○○○○

Highlights

Notes

FURZE HEDGE BARN

Height (m): 238m
OS Grid Reference: ST877379 • OS Grid Ref 10: ST8779137907
Flush bracket No: S2185

Date	Parking ★★★★★	Map Ref: 41

- Ascent Start Time
- Trig Time
- Descent Start Time
- Finish Time
- Ascent Duration
- Descent Duration
- Total Time
- Total Distance Covered
- No. Of Steps
- Companions

Weather

Difficulty to find ★★★★★

Enjoyment ○○○○○○○○○○
Views ○○○○○○○○○○
Difficulty ○○○○○○○○○○

Highlights

Notes

GIANTS GRAVE

Height (m): 250m
OS Grid Reference: SU165632 • OS Grid Ref 10: SU1658663209
Flush bracket No: S2173

Date	Parking ★★★★★	Map Ref: /42
Ascent Start Time		Trig Time
Descent Start Time		Finish Time
Ascent Duration	Descent Duration	Total Time
Total Distance Covered		No. Of Steps
Companions		

Weather		Difficulty to find ★★★★★

Enjoyment ○○○○○○○○○○
Views ○○○○○○○○○○
Difficulty ○○○○○○○○○○

Highlights

Notes

GROVELY CASTLE

Height (m): 156m
OS Grid Reference: SU047357 • OS Grid Ref 10: SU0474435730
Flush bracket No: S2203

Date	Parking	Map Ref: 43

Ascent Start Time	Trig Time

Descent Start Time	Finish Time

Ascent Duration	Descent Duration	Total Time

Total Distance Covered	No. Of Steps

Companions

Weather | Difficulty to find

- Enjoyment
- Views
- Difficulty

Highlights

Notes

GROVELY HILL

Height (m): 144m
OS Grid Reference: SU079327 • OS Grid Ref 10: SU0793932794
Flush bracket No: S2207

Date	Parking ★★★★★	Map Ref: 44

Ascent Start Time | **Trig Time**

Descent Start Time | **Finish Time**

Ascent Duration | **Descent Duration** | **Total Time**

Total Distance Covered | **No. Of Steps**

Companions

Weather | **Difficulty to find** ★★★★★

Enjoyment ○○○○○○○○○○
Views ○○○○○○○○○○
Difficulty ○○○○○○○○○○

Highlights

Notes

HACKPEN HILL

Height (m): 272m
OS Grid Reference: SU128743 • OS Grid Ref 10: SU1289774387
Flush bracket No: S2403

Date	Parking ☆☆☆☆☆	Map Ref: /45/
Ascent Start Time		Trig Time
Descent Start Time		Finish Time
Ascent Duration	Descent Duration	Total Time
Total Distance Covered		No. Of Steps
Companions		

Weather

Difficulty to find ☆☆☆☆☆

Enjoyment ○○○○○○○○○○
Views ○○○○○○○○○○
Difficulty ○○○○○○○○○○

Highlights

Notes

HORNINGSHAM

Height (m): 176m
OS Grid Reference: ST835409 • OS Grid Ref 10: ST8353140962
Flush bracket No: S2184

Date	Parking ★★★★★	Map Ref: 46

Ascent Start Time | **Trig Time**

Descent Start Time | **Finish Time**

Ascent Duration | **Descent Duration** | **Total Time**

Total Distance Covered | **No. Of Steps**

Companions

Weather | **Difficulty to find** ★★★★★

Enjoyment ○○○○○○○○○○
Views ○○○○○○○○○○
Difficulty ○○○○○○○○○○

Highlights

Notes

INHAM DOWN

Height (m): 196m
OS Grid Reference: SU225565 • OS Grid Ref 10: SU2258956598
Flush bracket No: S1907

Date	Parking ★★★★★	Map Ref: 47

Ascent Start Time	Trig Time

Descent Start Time	Finish Time

Ascent Duration	Descent Duration	Total Time

Total Distance Covered	No. Of Steps

Companions

Weather	Difficulty to find ★★★★★

Enjoyment ○○○○○○○○○
Views ○○○○○○○○○
Difficulty ○○○○○○○○○

Highlights

Notes

INKPEN HILL

Height (m): 290m
OS Grid Reference: SU353617 · OS Grid Ref 10: SU3539561759
Flush bracket No: S1910

| Date | Parking ★★★★★ | Map Ref: 48 |

Ascent Start Time | **Trig Time**

Descent Start Time | **Finish Time**

Ascent Duration | **Descent Duration** | **Total Time**

Total Distance Covered | **No. Of Steps**

Companions

Weather | **Difficulty to find** ★★★★★

Enjoyment ○○○○○○○○○○
Views ○○○○○○○○○○
Difficulty ○○○○○○○○○○

Highlights

Notes

KENTSWOOD

Height (m): 131m
OS Grid Reference: SU278345 • OS Grid Ref 10: SU2781534548
Flush bracket No: S2624

Date	Parking ★★★★★	Map Ref: 49

Ascent Start Time	Trig Time

Descent Start Time	Finish Time

Ascent Duration	Descent Duration	Total Time

Total Distance Covered	No. Of Steps

Companions

Weather	Difficulty to find ★★★★★

Enjoyment ○○○○○○○○○
Views ○○○○○○○○○
Difficulty ○○○○○○○○○

Highlights

Notes

KNIGHTON DOWN

Height (m): 147m
OS Grid Reference: SU127453 • OS Grid Ref 10: SU1277945349
Flush bracket No: S2172

Date	Parking ★★★★★	Map Ref: 50
Ascent Start Time		Trig Time
Descent Start Time		Finish Time
Ascent Duration	Descent Duration	Total Time
Total Distance Covered		No. Of Steps
Companions		
Weather		Difficulty to find ★★★★★

Enjoyment ○○○○○○○○○
Views ○○○○○○○○○
Difficulty ○○○○○○○○○

Highlights

Notes

KNOOK BARROW

Height (m): 189m
OS Grid Reference: ST957447 • OS Grid Ref 10: ST9575144794
Flush bracket No: S5913

Date	Parking ☆☆☆☆☆	Map Ref: 51

- Ascent Start Time
- Trig Time
- Descent Start Time
- Finish Time
- Ascent Duration
- Descent Duration
- Total Time
- Total Distance Covered
- No. Of Steps
- Companions
- Weather
- Difficulty to find ☆☆☆☆☆

Enjoyment ○○○○○○○○○○
Views ○○○○○○○○○○
Difficulty ○○○○○○○○○○

Highlights

Notes

LIDDINGTON CASTLE

Height (m): 278m
OS Grid Reference: SU209797 • OS Grid Ref 10: SU2098279753
Flush bracket No: S1268

Date	Parking ☆☆☆☆☆	Map Ref: 52
Ascent Start Time		Trig Time
Descent Start Time		Finish Time
Ascent Duration	Descent Duration	Total Time
Total Distance Covered		No. Of Steps
Companions		

Weather		Difficulty to find ☆☆☆☆☆

Enjoyment ○○○○○○○○○○
Views ○○○○○○○○○○
Difficulty ○○○○○○○○○○

Highlights

Notes

LITTLE HILL

Height (m): 249m
OS Grid Reference: ST868251 • OS Grid Ref 10: ST8686925132
Flush bracket No: S2227

Date	Parking	Map Ref: 53

Ascent Start Time — **Trig Time**

Descent Start Time — **Finish Time**

Ascent Duration — **Descent Duration** — **Total Time**

Total Distance Covered — **No. Of Steps**

Companions

Weather — **Difficulty to find**

Enjoyment

Views

Difficulty

Highlights

Notes

MARKET LAVINGTON

Height (m): 195m
OS Grid Reference: SU024530 • OS Grid Ref 10: SU0241353010
Flush bracket No: S5897

Date	Parking ☆☆☆☆☆	Map Ref: /54\
Ascent Start Time		Trig Time
Descent Start Time		Finish Time
Ascent Duration	Descent Duration	Total Time
Total Distance Covered		No. Of Steps
Companions		

Weather

Difficulty to find ☆☆☆☆☆

Enjoment ○○○○○○○○○○
Views ○○○○○○○○○○
Difficulty ○○○○○○○○○○

Highlights

Notes

MARTINSELL

Height (m): 290m
OS Grid Reference: SU178638 · OS Grid Ref 10: SU1783763868
Flush bracket No: S1500

Date	Parking ☆☆☆☆☆	Map Ref: /55

Ascent Start Time | **Trig Time**

Descent Start Time | **Finish Time**

Ascent Duration | **Descent Duration** | **Total Time**

Total Distance Covered | **No. Of Steps**

Companions

Weather | **Difficulty to find** ☆☆☆☆☆

Enjoyment ○○○○○○○○○○
Views ○○○○○○○○○○
Difficulty ○○○○○○○○○○

Highlights

Notes

MELBURY HILL

Height (m): 263m
OS Grid Reference: ST873197 • OS Grid Ref 10: ST8731719715
Flush bracket No: S6022

Date	Parking ★★★★★	Map Ref: /56\
Ascent Start Time		Trig Time
Descent Start Time		Finish Time
Ascent Duration	Descent Duration	Total Time
Total Distance Covered		No. Of Steps
Companions		
Weather		Difficulty to find ★★★★★

Enjoyment ○○○○○○○○○○
Views ○○○○○○○○○○
Difficulty ○○○○○○○○○○

Highlights

Notes

MILTON HILL

Height (m): 239m
OS Grid Reference: SU192584 • OS Grid Ref 10: SU1921758455
Flush bracket No: S1906

Date	Parking	☆☆☆☆☆	Map Ref: 57
Ascent Start Time		Trig Time	
Descent Start Time		Finish Time	
Ascent Duration	Descent Duration		Total Time
Total Distance Covered		No. Of Steps	
Companions			
Weather		Difficulty to find	☆☆☆☆☆

Enjoyment ○○○○○○○○○○
Views ○○○○○○○○○○
Difficulty ○○○○○○○○○○

Highlights

Notes

MORGANS HILL

Height (m): 260m
OS Grid Reference: SU029668 • OS Grid Ref 10: SU0296866873
Flush bracket No: S2501

Date	Parking ☆☆☆☆☆	Map Ref: /58\
Ascent Start Time		Trig Time
Descent Start Time		Finish Time
Ascent Duration	Descent Duration	Total Time
Total Distance Covered		No. Of Steps
Companions		

Weather — **Difficulty to find** ☆☆☆☆☆

Enjorment ○○○○○○○○○○
Views ○○○○○○○○○○
Difficulty ○○○○○○○○○○

Highlights

Notes

NEBO FARM

Height (m): 215m
OS Grid Reference: SU073764 • OS Grid Ref 10: SU0734376414
Flush bracket No: S2398

Date	Parking ☆☆☆☆☆	Map Ref: 59
Ascent Start Time		Trig Time
Descent Start Time		Finish Time
Ascent Duration	Descent Duration	Total Time
Total Distance Covered		No. Of Steps
Companions		

Weather	Difficulty to find ☆☆☆☆☆

- Enjoyment ○○○○○○○○○○
- Views ○○○○○○○○○○
- Difficulty ○○○○○○○○○○

Highlights

Notes

PALE ASH

Height (m): 170m
OS Grid Reference: SU076237 • OS Grid Ref 10: SU0763123731
Flush bracket No: S2602

Date	Parking ★★★★★	Map Ref: 60
Ascent Start Time		Trig Time
Descent Start Time		Finish Time
Ascent Duration	Descent Duration	Total Time
Total Distance Covered		No. Of Steps
Companions		

Weather

Difficulty to find ★★★★★

- Enjoyment ○○○○○○○○○○
- Views ○○○○○○○○○○
- Difficulty ○○○○○○○○○○

Highlights

Notes

PENNING FIELD

Height (m): 197m
OS Grid Reference: SU035231 • OS Grid Ref 10: SU0355023144
Flush bracket No: S2601

Date	Parking ☆☆☆☆☆	Map Ref: 61
Ascent Start Time		Trig Time
Descent Start Time		Finish Time
Ascent Duration	Descent Duration	Total Time
Total Distance Covered		No. Of Steps
Companions		

Weather | Difficulty to find ☆☆☆☆☆

Enjoyment ○○○○○○○○○○
Views ○○○○○○○○○○
Difficulty ○○○○○○○○○○

Highlights

Notes

PENTRIDGE HILL

Height (m): 185m
OS Grid Reference: SU040171 • OS Grid Ref 10: SU0403117140
Flush bracket No: S2590

Date	Parking ☆☆☆☆☆	Map Ref: 62
Ascent Start Time		Trig Time
Descent Start Time		Finish Time
Ascent Duration	Descent Duration	Total Time
Total Distance Covered		No. Of Steps
Companions		

Weather   Difficulty to find ☆☆☆☆☆

Enjoyment ○○○○○○○○○○
Views ○○○○○○○○○○
Difficulty ○○○○○○○○○○

Highlights

Notes

PICKED HILL

Height (m): 202m
OS Grid Reference: SU125610 • OS Grid Ref 10: SU1251261094
Flush bracket No: S1926

Date	Parking ★★★★★	Map Ref: 63
Ascent Start Time		Trig Time
Descent Start Time		Finish Time
Ascent Duration	Descent Duration	Total Time
Total Distance Covered		No. Of Steps
Companions		

Weather		Difficulty to find ★★★★★

- Enjoyment ○○○○○○○○○○
- Views ○○○○○○○○○○
- Difficulty ○○○○○○○○○○

Highlights

Notes

PICKPIT HILL

Height (m): 173m
OS Grid Reference: SU246500 • OS Grid Ref 10: SU2463550067
Flush bracket No: S1696

Date	Parking	Map Ref: 64

- Ascent Start Time
- Trig Time
- Descent Start Time
- Finish Time
- Ascent Duration
- Descent Duration
- Total Time
- Total Distance Covered
- No. Of Steps
- Companions

Weather

Difficulty to find

- Enjoyment
- Views
- Difficulty

Highlights

Notes

POULTON DOWNS

Height (m): 221m
OS Grid Reference: SU202724 • OS Grid Ref 10: SU2028072431
Flush bracket No: S6210

| Date | Parking | ☆☆☆☆☆ | Map Ref: /65\ |

- Ascent Start Time
- Trig Time
- Descent Start Time
- Finish Time
- Ascent Duration
- Descent Duration
- Total Time
- Total Distance Covered
- No. Of Steps
- Companions

Weather

Difficulty to find ☆☆☆☆☆

Enjoyment ○○○○○○○○○○
Views ○○○○○○○○○○
Difficulty ○○○○○○○○○○

Highlights

Notes

POUND BOTTOM

Height (m): 125m
OS Grid Reference: SU219172 • OS Grid Ref 10: SU2193017289
Flush bracket No: S2632

Date	Parking ☆☆☆☆☆	Map Ref: /66/
Ascent Start Time		Trig Time
Descent Start Time		Finish Time
Ascent Duration	Descent Duration	Total Time
Total Distance Covered		No. Of Steps
Companions		

| Weather | | Difficulty to find ☆☆☆☆☆ |

Enjoyment ○○○○○○○○○○
Views ○○○○○○○○○○
Difficulty ○○○○○○○○○○

Highlights

Notes

PRESHUTE

Height (m): 196m
OS Grid Reference: SU161697 • OS Grid Ref 10: SU1615569792
Flush bracket No: S2415

Date	Parking ☆☆☆☆☆	Map Ref: 67
Ascent Start Time		Trig Time
Descent Start Time		Finish Time
Ascent Duration	Descent Duration	Total Time
Total Distance Covered		No. Of Steps
Companions		
Weather		Difficulty to find ☆☆☆☆☆

Enjoyment ○○○○○○○○○○
Views ○○○○○○○○○○
Difficulty ○○○○○○○○○○

Highlights

Notes

PYT HOUSE

Height (m): 214m
OS Grid Reference: ST910290 • OS Grid Ref 10: ST9105629037
Flush bracket No: S2222

Date	Parking ★★★★★	Map Ref: 68

Ascent Start Time | **Trig Time**

Descent Start Time | **Finish Time**

Ascent Duration | **Descent Duration** | **Total Time**

Total Distance Covered | **No. Of Steps**

Companions

Weather | **Difficulty to find** ★★★★★

- Enjoyment ○○○○○○○○○○
- Views ○○○○○○○○○○
- Difficulty ○○○○○○○○○○

Highlights

Notes

QUARLEY CAMP

Height (m): 170m
OS Grid Reference: SU263424 • OS Grid Ref 10: SU2637042450
Flush bracket No: S1692

Date	Parking ☆☆☆☆☆	Map Ref: 69
Ascent Start Time		Trig Time
Descent Start Time		Finish Time
Ascent Duration	Descent Duration	Total Time
Total Distance Covered		No. Of Steps
Companions		

Weather		Difficulty to find ☆☆☆☆☆

Enjoyment ○○○○○○○○○○
Views ○○○○○○○○○○
Difficulty ○○○○○○○○○○

Highlights

Notes

REDHORN HILL

Height (m): 213m
OS Grid Reference: SU059551 • OS Grid Ref 10: SU0591155103
Flush bracket No: S1940

Date	Parking ☆☆☆☆☆	Map Ref: /70\

Ascent Start Time | **Trig Time**

Descent Start Time | **Finish Time**

Ascent Duration | **Descent Duration** | **Total Time**

Total Distance Covered | **No. Of Steps**

Companions

Weather | **Difficulty to find** ☆☆☆☆☆

Enjoyment ○○○○○○○○○○
Views ○○○○○○○○○○
Difficulty ○○○○○○○○○○

Highlights

Notes

ROYAL OAK

Height (m): 157m
OS Grid Reference: SU217252 • OS Grid Ref 10: SU2178225205
Flush bracket No: S2621

Date	Parking ★★★★★	Map Ref: 71
Ascent Start Time		Trig Time
Descent Start Time		Finish Time
Ascent Duration	Descent Duration	Total Time
Total Distance Covered		No. Of Steps
Companions		

Weather

Difficulty to find ★★★★★

Enjoyment ○○○○○○○○○○
Views ○○○○○○○○○○
Difficulty ○○○○○○○○○○

Highlights

Notes

SIDBURY

Height (m): 188m
OS Grid Reference: SU212508 • OS Grid Ref 10: SU2120950811
Flush bracket No: S1924

Date	Parking ☆☆☆☆☆	Map Ref: /72\
Ascent Start Time		Trig Time
Descent Start Time		Finish Time
Ascent Duration	Descent Duration	Total Time
Total Distance Covered		No. Of Steps
Companions		

| Weather | | Difficulty to find ☆☆☆☆☆ |

- Enjoyment ○○○○○○○○○○
- Views ○○○○○○○○○○
- Difficulty ○○○○○○○○○○

Highlights

Notes

SILK HILL

Height (m): 143m
OS Grid Reference: SU185468 • OS Grid Ref 10: SU1851646883
Flush bracket No: S1923

Date	Parking ★★★★★	Map Ref: /73\

Ascent Start Time	Trig Time

Descent Start Time	Finish Time

Ascent Duration	Descent Duration	Total Time

Total Distance Covered	No. Of Steps

Companions

Weather | **Difficulty to find** ★★★★★

Enjoyment ○○○○○○○○○○
Views ○○○○○○○○○○
Difficulty ○○○○○○○○○○

Highlights

Notes

STOCKTON

Height (m): 196m
OS Grid Reference: ST977355 • OS Grid Ref 10: ST9775135527
Flush bracket No: S2200

Date	Parking ★★★★★	Map Ref: 74

Ascent Start Time | **Trig Time**

Descent Start Time | **Finish Time**

Ascent Duration | **Descent Duration** | **Total Time**

Total Distance Covered | **No. Of Steps**

Companions

Weather | **Difficulty to find** ★★★★★

Enjoyment ○○○○○○○○○○
Views ○○○○○○○○○○
Difficulty ○○○○○○○○○○

Highlights

Notes

STRIDES ROW

Height (m): 81m
OS Grid Reference: SU246227 • OS Grid Ref 10: SU2464322716
Flush bracket No: S2631

Date	Parking	Map Ref: 75
Ascent Start Time		Trig Time
Descent Start Time		Finish Time
Ascent Duration	Descent Duration	Total Time
Total Distance Covered		No. Of Steps
Companions		
Weather		Difficulty to find

Enjoyment ○○○○○○○○○○
Views ○○○○○○○○○○
Difficulty ○○○○○○○○○○

Highlights

Notes

SUTTON DOWN

Height (m): 213m
OS Grid Reference: ST983261 • OS Grid Ref 10: ST9838926130
Flush bracket No: S2211

Date	Parking ★★★★★	Map Ref: /76/
Ascent Start Time		Trig Time
Descent Start Time		Finish Time
Ascent Duration	Descent Duration	Total Time
Total Distance Covered		No. Of Steps
Companions		
Weather		Difficulty to find ★★★★★

- Enjoyment ○○○○○○○○○○
- Views ○○○○○○○○○○
- Difficulty ○○○○○○○○○○

Highlights

Notes

TAN HILL

Height (m): 294m
OS Grid Reference: SU081646 • OS Grid Ref 10: SU0818664691
Flush bracket No: S2525

Date	Parking ★★★★★	Map Ref: /77\

Ascent Start Time	Trig Time

Descent Start Time	Finish Time

Ascent Duration	Descent Duration	Total Time

Total Distance Covered	No. Of Steps

Companions

Weather | **Difficulty to find** ★★★★★

Enjoyment ○○○○○○○○○○
Views ○○○○○○○○○○
Difficulty ○○○○○○○○○○

Highlights

Notes

TEFFONT DOWN

Height (m): 172m
OS Grid Reference: ST978340 • OS Grid Ref 10: ST9788534042
Flush bracket No: S2202

| Date | Parking ★★★★★ | Map Ref: /78\ |

Ascent Start Time | **Trig Time**

Descent Start Time | **Finish Time**

Ascent Duration | **Descent Duration** | **Total Time**

Total Distance Covered | **No. Of Steps**

Companions

Weather | **Difficulty to find** ★★★★★

Enjoyment ○○○○○○○○○
Views ○○○○○○○○○
Difficulty ○○○○○○○○○

Highlights

Notes

TERRACE HILL

Height (m): 196m
OS Grid Reference: SU232638 • OS Grid Ref 10: SU2329663838
Flush bracket No: S1911

Date	Parking ★★★★★	Map Ref: 79

Ascent Start Time | **Trig Time**

Descent Start Time | **Finish Time**

Ascent Duration | **Descent Duration** | **Total Time**

Total Distance Covered | **No. Of Steps**

Companions

Weather | **Difficulty to find** ★★★★★

Enjoyment ○○○○○○○○○○
Views ○○○○○○○○○○
Difficulty ○○○○○○○○○○

Highlights

Notes

THRUXTON DOWN

Height (m): 174m
OS Grid Reference: SU246453 • OS Grid Ref 10: SU2464945313
Flush bracket No: S1697

Date	Parking ★★★★★	Map Ref: /80\

Ascent Start Time	Trig Time

Descent Start Time	Finish Time

Ascent Duration	Descent Duration	Total Time

Total Distance Covered	No. Of Steps

Companions

Weather	Difficulty to find ★★★★★

Enjoyment ○○○○○○○○○○
Views ○○○○○○○○○○
Difficulty ○○○○○○○○○○

Highlights

Notes

TITTLE PATH HILL

Height (m): 242m
OS Grid Reference: ST892256 • OS Grid Ref 10: ST8925625628
Flush bracket No: S2224

Date	Parking ☆☆☆☆☆	Map Ref: /81\
Ascent Start Time		Trig Time
Descent Start Time		Finish Time
Ascent Duration	Descent Duration	Total Time
Total Distance Covered		No. Of Steps
Companions		

WeatherDifficulty to find ☆☆☆☆☆

Enjoyment ○○○○○○○○○○
Views ○○○○○○○○○○
Difficulty ○○○○○○○○○○

Highlights

Notes

TRIPLE PLANTATION

Height (m): 143m
OS Grid Reference: SU178504 • OS Grid Ref 10: SU1788250483
Flush bracket No: S1928

Date	Parking ★★★★★	Map Ref: /82\
Ascent Start Time		Trig Time
Descent Start Time		Finish Time
Ascent Duration	Descent Duration	Total Time
Total Distance Covered		No. Of Steps
Companions		
Weather		Difficulty to find ★★★★★

- Enjoyment ◯◯◯◯◯◯◯◯◯◯
- Views ◯◯◯◯◯◯◯◯◯◯
- Difficulty ◯◯◯◯◯◯◯◯◯◯

Highlights

Notes

TROW DOWN

Height (m): 244m
OS Grid Reference: ST971217 • OS Grid Ref 10: ST9714321717
Flush bracket No: S2600

Date	Parking ☆☆☆☆☆	Map Ref: /83\
Ascent Start Time		Trig Time
Descent Start Time		Finish Time
Ascent Duration	Descent Duration	Total Time
Total Distance Covered		No. Of Steps
Companions		

Weather | Difficulty to find ☆☆☆☆☆

Enjoyment ○○○○○○○○○○
Views ○○○○○○○○○○
Difficulty ○○○○○○○○○○

Highlights

Notes

UPTON COW DOWN

Height (m): 200m
OS Grid Reference: ST878492 • OS Grid Ref 10: ST8787049209
Flush bracket No: S2523

Date	Parking ★★★★★	Map Ref: 84

Ascent Start Time	Trig Time

Descent Start Time	Finish Time

Ascent Duration	Descent Duration	Total Time

Total Distance Covered	No. Of Steps

Companions

Weather	Difficulty to find ★★★★★

Enjoyment ○○○○○○○○○○
Views ○○○○○○○○○○
Difficulty ○○○○○○○○○○

Highlights

Notes

WADEN HILL

Height (m): 192m
OS Grid Reference: SU104691 · OS Grid Ref 10: SU1040669180
Flush bracket No: S2414

Date	Parking ★★★★★	Map Ref: /85\
Ascent Start Time		Trig Time
Descent Start Time		Finish Time
Ascent Duration	Descent Duration	Total Time
Total Distance Covered		No. Of Steps
Companions		
Weather		Difficulty to find ★★★★★

Enjoyment ○○○○○○○○○○
Views ○○○○○○○○○○
Difficulty ○○○○○○○○○○

Highlights

Notes

WADSWICK

Height (m): 138m
OS Grid Reference: ST844677 • OS Grid Ref 10: ST8442467728
Flush bracket No: S2486

Date	Parking ☆☆☆☆☆	Map Ref: 86
Ascent Start Time		Trig Time
Descent Start Time		Finish Time
Ascent Duration	Descent Duration	Total Time
Total Distance Covered		No. Of Steps
Companions		

Weather | Difficulty to find ☆☆☆☆☆

Enjoyment ○○○○○○○○○○
Views ○○○○○○○○○○
Difficulty ○○○○○○○○○○

Highlights

Notes

WARMINSTER BOTTOM

Height (m): 189m
OS Grid Reference: ST982506 • OS Grid Ref 10: ST9824250649
Flush bracket No: S1925

Date	Parking ☆☆☆☆☆	Map Ref: /87\
Ascent Start Time	Trig Time	
Descent Start Time	Finish Time	
Ascent Duration	Descent Duration	Total Time
Total Distance Covered		No. Of Steps
Companions		
Weather	Difficulty to find ☆☆☆☆☆	

Enjoyment ○○○○○○○○○○
Views ○○○○○○○○○○
Difficulty ○○○○○○○○○○

Highlights

Notes

WEST HILL

Height (m): 198m
OS Grid Reference: SU006353 • OS Grid Ref 10: SU0069935322
Flush bracket No: S2201

Date	Parking ★★★★★	Map Ref: /88\
Ascent Start Time		Trig Time
Descent Start Time		Finish Time
Ascent Duration	Descent Duration	Total Time
Total Distance Covered		No. Of Steps
Companions		

Weather		Difficulty to find ★★★★★

Enjoyment ○○○○○○○○○○
Views ○○○○○○○○○○
Difficulty ○○○○○○○○○○

Highlights

Notes

WEST KNOYLE TUMULUS

Height (m): 228m
OS Grid Reference: ST865327 • OS Grid Ref 10: ST8656732734
Flush bracket No: S2226

Date	Parking ★★★★★	Map Ref: 89
Ascent Start Time		Trig Time
Descent Start Time		Finish Time
Ascent Duration	Descent Duration	Total Time
Total Distance Covered		No. Of Steps
Companions		
Weather		Difficulty to find ★★★★★

Enjoyment ○○○○○○○○○○
Views ○○○○○○○○○○
Difficulty ○○○○○○○○○○

Highlights

Notes

WEST WELLOW

Height (m): 45m
OS Grid Reference: SU284188 • OS Grid Ref 10: SU2846518836
Flush bracket No: S2721

Date	Parking	★★★★★	Map Ref: 90

Ascent Start Time		Trig Time	
Descent Start Time		Finish Time	
Ascent Duration	Descent Duration		Total Time
Total Distance Covered		No. Of Steps	
Companions			

Weather		Difficulty to find	★★★★★

Enjoyment ○○○○○○○○○○
Views ○○○○○○○○○○
Difficulty ○○○○○○○○○○

Highlights

Notes

WESTBURY DOWN

Height (m): 230m
OS Grid Reference: ST901511 · OS Grid Ref 10: ST9011251135
Flush bracket No: S1531

Date	Parking	Map Ref: 91
Ascent Start Time		Trig Time
Descent Start Time		Finish Time
Ascent Duration	Descent Duration	Total Time
Total Distance Covered		No. Of Steps
Companions		
Weather		Difficulty to find

Enjoyment
Views
Difficulty

Highlights

Notes

WEXCOMBE DOWN

Height (m): 267m
OS Grid Reference: SU277577 • OS Grid Ref 10: SU2776857735
Flush bracket No: S1909

Date	Parking ★★★★★	Map Ref: 92

Ascent Start Time	Trig Time

Descent Start Time	Finish Time

Ascent Duration	Descent Duration	Total Time

Total Distance Covered	No. Of Steps

Companions

Weather	Difficulty to find ★★★★★

- Enjoyment ○○○○○○○○○○
- Views ○○○○○○○○○○
- Difficulty ○○○○○○○○○○

Highlights

Notes

WHITE SHEET CASTLE

Height (m): 245m
OS Grid Reference: ST804347 • OS Grid Ref 10: ST8048634714
Flush bracket No: S2228

Date	Parking ★★★★★	Map Ref: 93
Ascent Start Time	Trig Time	
Descent Start Time	Finish Time	
Ascent Duration	Descent Duration	Total Time
Total Distance Covered		No. Of Steps
Companions		

Weather	Difficulty to find ★★★★★

Enjoyment ○○○○○○○○○○
Views ○○○○○○○○○○
Difficulty ○○○○○○○○○○

Highlights

Notes

WHITE SHEET HILL

Height (m): 243m
OS Grid Reference: ST944242 • OS Grid Ref 10: ST9440324256
Flush bracket No: S2223

Date	Parking ☆☆☆☆☆	Map Ref: /94/

Ascent Start Time | **Trig Time**

Descent Start Time | **Finish Time**

Ascent Duration | **Descent Duration** | **Total Time**

Total Distance Covered | **No. Of Steps**

Companions

Weather | **Difficulty to find** ☆☆☆☆☆

Enjoyment ○○○○○○○○○○
Views ○○○○○○○○○○
Difficulty ○○○○○○○○○○

Highlights

Notes

WICK DOWN

Height (m): 115m
OS Grid Reference: SU136215 • OS Grid Ref 10: SU1360021556
Flush bracket No: S2607

Date	Parking ★★★★★	Map Ref: /95\

Ascent Start Time | **Trig Time**

Descent Start Time | **Finish Time**

Ascent Duration | **Descent Duration** | **Total Time**

Total Distance Covered | **No. Of Steps**

Companions

Weather | **Difficulty to find** ★★★★★

- Enjoyment ○○○○○○○○○○
- Views ○○○○○○○○○○
- Difficulty ○○○○○○○○○○

Highlights

Notes

WICK DOWN

Height (m): 185m
OS Grid Reference: SU261530 • OS Grid Ref 10: SU2610453032
Flush bracket No: S1927

Date	Parking ★★★★★	Map Ref: /96\
Ascent Start Time		Trig Time
Descent Start Time		Finish Time
Ascent Duration	Descent Duration	Total Time
Total Distance Covered		No. Of Steps
Companions		

Weather		Difficulty to find ★★★★★

- Enjoyment ○○○○○○○○○○
- Views   ○○○○○○○○○○
- Difficulty ○○○○○○○○○○

Highlights

Notes

WINGREEN

Height (m): 278m
OS Grid Reference: ST925206 • OS Grid Ref 10: ST9250620645
Flush bracket No: S1503

Date	Parking ☆☆☆☆☆	Map Ref: 97
Ascent Start Time		Trig Time
Descent Start Time		Finish Time
Ascent Duration	Descent Duration	Total Time
Total Distance Covered		No. Of Steps
Companions		
Weather	Difficulty to find ☆☆☆☆☆	

Enjoyment ○○○○○○○○○○
Views   ○○○○○○○○○○
Difficulty ○○○○○○○○○○

Highlights

Notes

WINTERSLOW

Height (m): 163m
OS Grid Reference: SU242336 • OS Grid Ref 10: SU2420133623
Flush bracket No: S2604

Date	Parking ★★★★★	Map Ref: /98\
Ascent Start Time		Trig Time
Descent Start Time		Finish Time
Ascent Duration	Descent Duration	Total Time
Total Distance Covered		No. Of Steps
Companions		

Weather		Difficulty to find ★★★★★

- Enjoyment ○○○○○○○○○○
- Views ○○○○○○○○○○
- Difficulty ○○○○○○○○○○

Highlights

Notes

WOODFORD

Height (m): 156m
OS Grid Reference: SU101355 • OS Grid Ref 10: SU1012735524
Flush bracket No: S2208

Date	Parking ☆☆☆☆☆	Map Ref: 99

Ascent Start Time | **Trig Time**

Descent Start Time | **Finish Time**

Ascent Duration | **Descent Duration** | **Total Time**

Total Distance Covered | **No. Of Steps**

Companions

Weather | **Difficulty to find** ☆☆☆☆☆

Enjoyment ○○○○○○○○○
Views ○○○○○○○○○
Difficulty ○○○○○○○○○

Highlights

Notes

WORTHY HILL FARM

Height (m): 135m
OS Grid Reference: SU019881 • OS Grid Ref 10: SU0198988149
Flush bracket No: S2420

Date	Parking ★★★★★	Map Ref: /100\
Ascent Start Time		Trig Time
Descent Start Time		Finish Time
Ascent Duration	Descent Duration	Total Time
Total Distance Covered		No. Of Steps
Companions		

Weather

Difficulty to find ★★★★★

- Enjoyment ○○○○○○○○○○
- Views ○○○○○○○○○○
- Difficulty ○○○○○○○○○○

Highlights

Notes

WORTON

Height (m): 85m
OS Grid Reference: ST987563 • OS Grid Ref 10: ST9879956357
Flush bracket No: S2487

Date	Parking ☆☆☆☆☆	Map Ref: /101\
Ascent Start Time	Trig Time	
Descent Start Time	Finish Time	
Ascent Duration	Descent Duration	Total Time
Total Distance Covered		No. Of Steps
Companions		

Weather	Difficulty to find ☆☆☆☆☆

Enjoyment ○○○○○○○○○○
Views ○○○○○○○○○○
Difficulty ○○○○○○○○○○

Highlights

Notes

WROUGHTON

Height (m): 208m
OS Grid Reference: SU128794 • OS Grid Ref 10: SU1286579420
Flush bracket No: S6280

Date	Parking ★★★★★	Map Ref: /102\
Ascent Start Time		Trig Time
Descent Start Time		Finish Time
Ascent Duration	Descent Duration	Total Time
Total Distance Covered		No. Of Steps
Companions		

Weather | Difficulty to find ★★★★★

Enjoyment ○○○○○○○○○○
Views ○○○○○○○○○○
Difficulty ○○○○○○○○○○

Highlights

Notes

YARNBURY CASTLE

Height (m): 167m
OS Grid Reference: SU037402 • OS Grid Ref 10: SU0372640287
Flush bracket No: S2170

Date	Parking ☆☆☆☆☆	Map Ref: /103\
Ascent Start Time	Trig Time	
Descent Start Time	Finish Time	
Ascent Duration	Descent Duration	Total Time
Total Distance Covered		No. Of Steps
Companions		
Weather	Difficulty to find ☆☆☆☆☆	

Enjoyment ○○○○○○○○○
Views ○○○○○○○○○
Difficulty ○○○○○○○○○

Highlights

Notes

Equipment Checklist

Why not join the HIKING BUDDIES UK
EST 2022

We are a community for outdoor enthusiasts who wish to venture out and connect with others who share their interests in the breathtaking areas the UK has to offer.

We're working hard behind the scenes to bring you discounted trips in the UK and abroad as well as high quality clothing that caters for all seasons.

> I founded this group because I found solace in adventure and meeting new people while coping with mental health challenges.
> Hiking and climbing mountains helped me, but I wanted to create a community to support others, who may feel hesitant to embark on such journeys alone.
>
> *Marlon*

- facebook.com/groups/hikingbuddiesuk
- instagram.com/hikingbuddiesuk
- tiktok.com/@hikingbuddiesuk
- youtube.com/@hikingbuddiesuk

Ready to record your next adventure?

Keeping a logbook is a fantastic way of recording your memories - and we have published a number of adventure logbooks on Amazon. Simply scan the QR code to find out more!

THE
HAMPSHIRE
& ISLE OF WIGHT
TRIG BAGGER
CHALLENGE
LOGBOOK
138
TAKE ON THE HAMPSHIRE TRIG BAGGER CHALLENGE!

THE
WILTSHIRE
TRIG
BAGGER
CHALLENGE LOGBOOK
103
TAKE ON THE WILTSHIRE TRIG BAGGER CHALLENGE

THE
PEAK DISTRICT
ETHELS
PEAK BAGGER LOGBOOK
TAKE ON THE ETHELS CHALLENGE!

THE
DEVON
TRIG
BAGGER
CHALLENGE LOGBOOK
217
TAKE ON THE DEVON TRIG BAGGER CHALLENGE!

THE COMPLETE
SCOTLAND
GRAHAMS
PEAK BAGGERS LOGBOOK
TAKE ON THE SCOTTISH GRAHAMS CHALLENGE

DARTMOOR
PEAK BAGGER
LOGBOOK
TAKE ON THE PEAK BAGGER CHALLENGE
WITH ALL 82 BEAUTIFUL PEAKS IN DARTMOOR

THE
DORSET
TRIG
BAGGER
CHALLENGE LOGBOOK
102
TAKE ON THE DORSET TRIG BAGGER CHALLENGE

THE
COUNTY DURHAM
TRIG
BAGGER
81
TAKE ON THE COUNTY DURHAM TRIG CHALLENGE

109
PEAK DISTRICT
TRIG BAGGERS
LOGBOOK
WITH QR CODES FOR MAPS
& OS GRID REFERENCES

THE COMPLETE
SCOTLAND
MUNROS
PEAK BAGGER LOGBOOK
TAKE ON THE MUNRO CHALLENGE

111
THE
YORKSHIRE
DALES
TRIG BAGGERS
LOGBOOK
WITH QR CODES FOR MAPS
& OS GRID REFERENCES

THE
SOMERSET
TRIG
BAGGER
CHALLENGE LOGBOOK
TAKE ON THE SOMERSET TRIG CHALLENGE

Printed in Great Britain
by Amazon